TRICERATOPS
WOULD **NOT** make a GOOD
NINJA

by Lisa Katzenberger   illustrated by Steph Calvert

PICTURE WINDOW BOOKS
a capstone imprint

RÉSUMÉ

MILLIE TRICERATOPS

50 Frill Lane
Big Horn, NT 40052

LENGTH	30 feet (9 meters)
HEIGHT	10 ft (3m)
WEIGHT	4-6 tons
NECK FRILL	spanned 6 ft (1.8m)
EXPERIENCE AS A NINJA	It's a long story.
REFERENCE	NOT this gal →

For Ryan and Sydney – L.K.

For Phil - Your cardboard armor, paper swords, and boundless creativity are an inspiration. You are amazing. – Steph

Dinosaur Daydreams is published by
Picture Window Books, a Capstone Imprint
1710 Roe Crest Drive
North Mankato, MN 56003
www.mycapstone.com

Library of Congress Cataloging-in-Publication data is available on the Library of Congress website.

ISBN: 978-1-5158-2127-4 (library binding)
ISBN: 978-1-5158-2131-1 (paperback)
ISBN: 978-1-5158-2139-7 (eBook PDF)

Summary: A new ninja school just opened, and Millie Triceratops is ready to enroll! It can't be that hard to be quiet, sneak around, and kick hard, can it? Millie might be in for quite the surprise!

Image Credit: Capstone: Jon Hughes, 23

Editor: CHRISTIANNE JONES
Designer: ASHLEE SUKER
Illustrator: STEPH CALVERT

Printed and bound in the USA.
010853S18

Hi, I'm **MILLIE** Triceratops, and I love new adventures. I've tried lots of different activities, but nothing has worked out. I recently tried to be a ninja. It did not go well.

Last week I was walking across the hot, flat plains when I saw a new sign. **NINJA SCHOOL!** I'd always wanted to be a ninja, so I joined right away.

Ninjas took their work VERY seriously. They
spent a lot of time studying their enemies.
I grabbed a book and started studying. Wait . . .
what was I going to do again? I forgot that
I am easily distracted.

HOOVES

8

I really wanted to be a great ninja, so I practiced my skills. Ninjas were quiet and nimble. I tried to tiptoe. But my heavy feet made tons of noise. Clearly, I needed to work on this skill.

Day 2: sneaking

NINJA SCHOOL
PROGRESS REPORT
FOR: Millie the TriceR...

DAY 1	DAY 2	DAY 3	DAY 4	DAY 5
study	sneaking you tried			

Ninjas were great at hiding. They would spring out from shadows for surprise attacks. I tried to hide behind a car, but my horns and frill wouldn't cooperate.

Like a ninja, I tried to stay alert. I kept an eye out for my greatest enemy, the T-Rex. **GOOD NEWS!** I was really good at keeping watch because my eyes are on the sides of my head. **BAD NEWS!** I was not as good at staying awake.

NINJA SCHOOL PROGRESS REPORT

FOR: Millie the Triceratops

DAY 1	DAY 2	DAY 3	DAY 4	DAY 5	DAY 6	DAY 7
study	sneaking you tried	hiding NEEDS IMPROVEMENT	being alert			

Ninjas usually work alone, but triceratops work together in herds. So when my friends showed up to cheer me on, I had to quickly shoo them away. However, I did like the attention.

We went to a big field to practice spying and hiding. I thought I heard something, so I darted behind a big bunch of bushes. But it wasn't long before I ate all the leaves. After all, I am an herbivore. What did you expect?

I knew it was time to try the most powerful ninja skills of all – jumps and kicks. I took a running start . . .

leaped into the air . . .

and flopped right onto my belly.
My legs are just too short.

I guess being a ninja just wasn't for me. I went back to ninja school to turn in my uniform. On my way out, I saw another sign – **BASEBALL TRYOUTS!**

I bet I'll be **GREAT** at that!

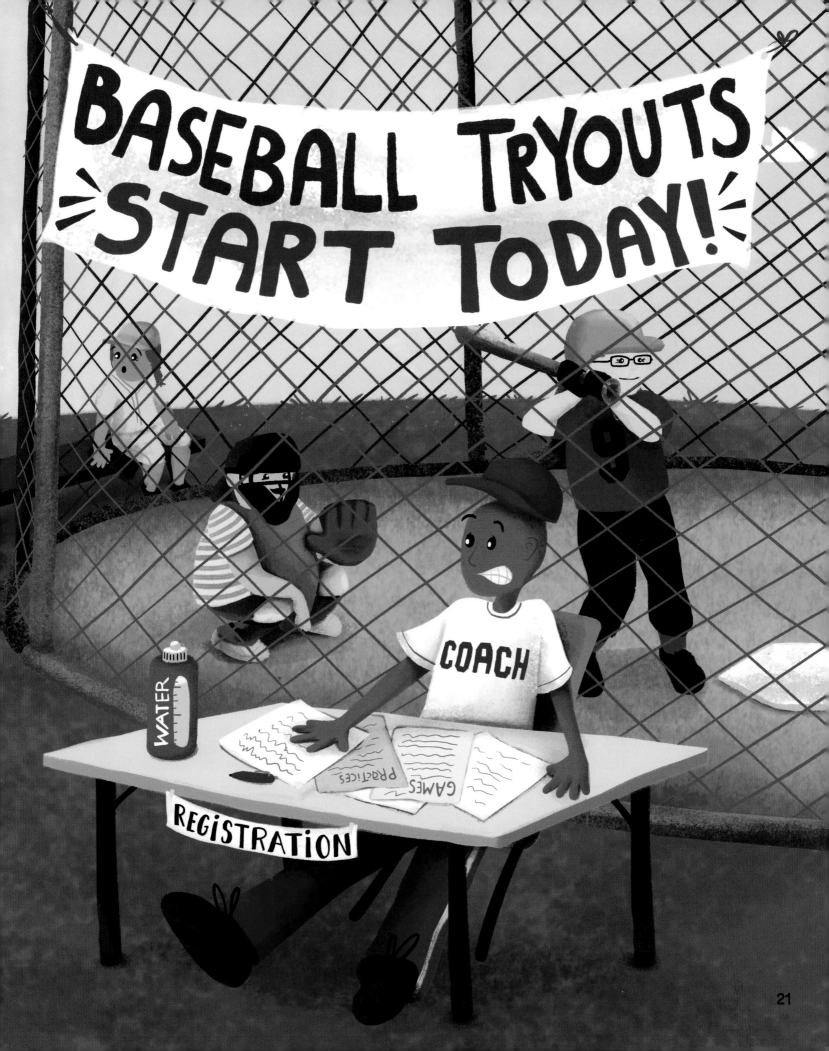

DINO DIG

The answer to each question below is hidden in the art. Each answer is one word or number. Dig through the story until you find the answer. Good luck!

1. Which state did most triceratops live in? (page 5)

2. Triceratops didn't have toes. What did they have instead? (page 8)

3. Triceratops had columns of sharp teeth. What were those columns called? (page 16)

4. Triceratops legs were short, so they couldn't run very fast. A tricertops was as fast as what modern-day animal? (page 18)

5. A triceratops' horns and bony frill were used for protection. Which dinosaur was the triceratops' greatest enemy? (page 13)

MORE TRICERATOPS FACTS

» Of all the land animals, triceratops' head is one of the largest discovered. Its head took up one-third of its entire body!

» Juvenile triceratops hung out together in small groups called herds. It wasn't until they became adults that they traveled on their own.

» Triceratops lived during the late Cretaceous Period (around 65 million years ago). They were one of the last remaining dinosaurs on Earth.

» When a triceratops' tooth fell out, a replacement tooth was ready to drop in its spot. Triceratops could have anywhere from 400-800 teeth!

» Triceratops means "three-horned face."

DINO DISCUSSION

1. Would you rather be a ninja or a dinosaur? Why?

2. What characteristics made Millie a bad ninja? Do you think she'll be a good baseball player?

3. What job would be a good fit for Millie?

DINO GLOSSARY

frill – a bony collar around the neck of an animal

herbivore – an animal that eats only plants

hooved – having hooves

NINJA GLOSSARY

alert – being watchful

distracted – drew attention to something else

nimble – quick and light

skills – things you learn from training or practice